SEA LIONS

by JoAnn Early Macken

Reading consultant: Susan Nations, M.Ed., author/literacy coach/consultant

WEEKLY WR READER®
EARLY LEARNING LIBRARY

Please visit our web site at: **www.earlyliteracy.cc**
For a free color catalog describing Weekly Reader® Early Learning Library's list of high-quality books, call 1-877-445-5824 (USA) or 1-800-387-3178 (Canada). Weekly Reader® Early Learning Library's fax: (414) 336-0164.

Library of Congress Cataloging-in-Publication Data

Macken, JoAnn Early, 1953-
    Sea lions / by JoAnn Early Macken.
      p. cm. — (Animals I see at the zoo)
    Summary: Photographs and simple text introduce the physical characteristics
and behavior of sea lions, one of many animals kept in zoos.
    Includes bibliographical references and index.
    ISBN 0-8368-3274-4 (lib. bdg.)
    ISBN 0-8368-3287-6 (softcover)
    1. Sea lions—Juvenile literature. 2. Zoo animals—Juvenile literature. [1. Sea lions.
2. Zoo animals.] I. Title.
    QL737.P63M284   2002
    599.79'75—dc21
                                             2002016873

This edition first published in 2002 by
Weekly Reader® Early Learning Library
330 West Olive Street, Suite 100
Milwaukee, WI 53212 USA

Art direction: Tammy Gruenewald
Production: Susan Ashley
Photo research: Diane Laska-Swanke
Graphic design: Katherine A. Goedheer

Photo credits: Cover, title, pp. 5, 11, 15, 17, 21 © James P. Rowan; p. 7 © Richard Herrmann/Visuals Unlimited; p. 9 © Hal Beral/Visuals Unlimited; p. 13 © Walt Anderson/Visuals Unlimited; p. 19 © Joe McDonald/Visuals Unlimited

Printed in the United States of America

1 2 3 4 5 6 7 8 9 06 05 04 03 02

Note to Educators and Parents

Reading is such an exciting adventure for young children! They are beginning to integrate their oral language skills with written language. To encourage children along the path to early literacy, books must be colorful, engaging, and interesting; they should invite the young reader to explore both the print and the pictures.

Animals I See at the Zoo is a new series designed to help children read about twelve fascinating animals. In each book, young readers will learn interesting facts about the featured animal.

Each book is specially designed to support the young reader in the reading process. The familiar topics are appealing to young children and invite them to read — and re-read — again and again. The full-color photographs and enhanced text further support the student during the reading process.

In addition to serving as wonderful picture books in schools, libraries, homes, and other places where children learn to love reading, these books are specifically intended to be read within an instructional guided reading group. This small group setting allows beginning readers to work with a fluent adult model as they make meaning from the text. After children develop fluency with the text and content, the book can be read independently. Children and adults alike will find these books supportive, engaging, and fun!

— Susan Nations, M.Ed., author, literacy coach, and consultant in literacy development

I like to go to the zoo. I see sea lions at the zoo.

Sea lions swim
and dive. They
use their front
flippers like oars.
They steer with
their back flippers.

flippers

They dive to look for food. They feel for food with their **whiskers**.

whiskers

Sea lions have fat under their skin to keep them warm. Their smooth shape helps them swim fast.

Sea lions rest on land. They can walk on their flippers.

Sea lions stay
in large groups.
They sleep in piles
to stay warm.

Sea lions are noisy. They bark, and they roar like lions.

Like lions, some male sea lions have **manes**. Can you see how they got their name?

mane

I like to see
sea lions at the
zoo. Do you?

Glossary

manes — long hair on some animals' necks

steer — to direct the course of something

whiskers — long, bristly hair on an animal's face

For More Information

Books

Arnold, Caroline. *Sea Lion*. New York: Morrow Junior Books, 1994.

Shahan, Sherry. *Feeding Time at the Zoo*. New York: Random House, 2000.

van Eerbeek, Ton. *The World of Baby Animals*. New York: Sterling Publishing, 2001.

Web Sites

Sea World/Busch Gardens Animal Information Database

www.seaworld.org/Pinnipeds/sealion.html

For a California sea lion illustration and facts

Seal Conservation Society

www.pinnipeds.fsnet.co.uk/species/species.htm

For photos and facts about seals, sea lions, and walruses

Index

About the Author

JoAnn Early Macken is the author of a rhyming picture book, *Cats on Judy*, and *Animal Worlds*, a series of nonfiction picture books about animals and their habitats. Her poems have been published or accepted by *Ladybug*, *Spider*, *Highlights for Children*, and an anthology, *Stories from Where We Live: The Great Lakes*. A winner of the Barbara Juster Esbensen 2000 Poetry Teaching Award, she teaches poetry writing. She lives in Wisconsin with her husband and their two sons.